The Future of Artificial Intelligence in Digital Marketing

Artificial Intelligence Reshaping the Landscape of Digital Marketing

James Brandy

TABLE OF CONTENTS

INTRODUCTION

Artificial Intelligence (AI) is reshaping the landscape of digital marketing, ushering in an era of unprecedented possibilities and transformative strategies. In this book, "The Future of Artificial Intelligence in Digital Marketing," we embark on a journey to explore the intricate fusion of cutting-edge technology and marketing innovation.

Unveiling the Potential

As businesses navigate the digital realm, AI emerges as a powerful ally, offering insights, automation, and personalization that redefine marketing paradigms. From predictive analytics to Chabot and beyond, AI's impact is profound, revolutionizing how brands connect with their audiences.

Crafting Personalized Experiences

The heart of this exploration lies in the realm of personalized experiences. The book delves into how AI tailors content, messages, and interactions, ensuring that each engagement is not just a touchpoint but a personalized journey. It illuminates the techniques and technologies that enable businesses to resonate with their customers on a deeper, more meaningful level.

Navigating Ethical Horizons

However, with great power comes responsibility. We scrutinize the ethical considerations surrounding AI in digital marketing, emphasizing the importance of transparency and ethical practices. The future demands a delicate balance between innovation and ethical stewardship.

Roadmap for Implementation

Practicality is key. This book is not just a theoretical exploration but a guide for implementing AI strategies in real-world marketing scenarios. Through case studies and hands-on insights, businesses can unlock the full potential of AI, fostering a competitive edge in the dynamic digital landscape.

Join us in unraveling the future of digital marketing, where AI is not just a tool but a catalyst for unparalleled growth and engagement.

CHAPTER ONE

Overview of Artificial Intelligence (AI) in Digital Marketing

In recent years, the integration of Artificial Intelligence (AI) in digital marketing has ushered in a new era of innovation and efficiency. This chapter explores the significance and evolution of AI technologies within the realm of digital marketing.

1.1 Significance of AI in Digital Marketing

Artificial Intelligence has proven to be a game-changer for marketers, offering unprecedented capabilities to analyze vast amounts of data, automate processes, and enhance decision-making. Its potential lies in its ability to optimize marketing strategies, personalize customer experiences, and ultimately drive more effective and targeted campaigns.

1.2 Evolution of AI Technologies in Marketing

The evolution of AI in digital marketing has been marked by continuous advancements and innovations. From predictive analytics to machine learning algorithms, AI has transformed how marketers understand consumer behavior and tailor their approaches accordingly. As AI technologies continue to mature, they are likely to substantially change both marketing strategies and customer behaviors

This chapter sets the stage for a deeper exploration into the various facets of AI in digital marketing, highlighting its transformative impact and setting the tone for the future chapters to delve into specific applications and implications.

CHAPTER TWO

Foundations of AI in Digital Marketing

2.1 Basics of AI and Machine Learning

To fathom the eventual fate of computerized reasoning in advanced advertising, it is crucial to establish a solid understanding of the basics. Artificial Intelligence encompasses a broad field, but at its core, it involves the development of algorithms that can mimic human intelligence. Machine Learning, a group of AI, empowers systems to learn and improve from experience without definite programming.

2.1.1 The Essence of AI

AI is characterized by its ability to analyze data, recognize patterns, and make decisions autonomously. Understanding the principles of supervised and unsupervised learning provides the groundwork for comprehending AI's role in marketing strategies.

2.1.2 Machine Learning Fundamentals

Machine Learning, a driving force behind AI in marketing, relies on algorithms that enable systems to learn from data. Whether through supervised learning, where models are trained on labeled data, or unsupervised learning, where patterns are noticed without predefined labels, the fundamentals of ML form the backbone of AI applications in marketing.

2.2 How AI Algorithms Work in Marketing Contexts

AI algorithms play a pivotal role in shaping marketing strategies. They enhance the accuracy of focusing on, streamline decision-making processes, and optimize campaign performance.

2.2.1 Personalization through AI

AI algorithms investigate customer information to create personalized experiences. From recommending products based on past behavior to tailoring content, personalization powered by AI enhances customer engagement and satisfaction.

2.2.2 Predictive Analytics in Marketing

AI's predictive capabilities enable marketers to forecast future trends, customer behaviors, and campaign outcomes. By analyzing historical data, AI algorithms empower marketers to make informed decisions, ultimately improving the effectiveness of their initiatives.

This chapter establishes the foundational knowledge required to delve into the practical applications of AI in digital marketing, paving the way for a deeper exploration in subsequent chapters.

3.1 Analysis of Existing AI Applications in Marketing

The ongoing scene of advanced promotion is significantly impacted by the reconciliation of Computerized reasoning (artificial intelligence). This chapter offers an in-depth analysis of the existing AI applications that have reshaped marketing strategies.

3.1.1 Customer Segmentation and Targeting

AI has revolutionized customer segmentation by enabling marketers to analyze vast datasets and identify nuanced segments. This not only enhances targeting accuracy but also allows for personalized content delivery, improving overall campaign effectiveness.

3.1.2 Chabot and Conversational Marketing

AI-powered Chabot have become invaluable assets in digital marketing. They engage with customers in real-time, providing personalized recommendations, answering queries, and enhancing the overall customer experience. These not only improve customer satisfaction but also streamline communication processes for businesses.

3.2 Case Studies Illustrating Successful Implementations

Real-world case studies provide concrete examples of how AI has been successfully implemented in digital marketing, yielding tangible results.

3.2.1 Netflix: Personalized Content Recommendations

Netflix utilizes AI algorithms to analyze user viewing patterns and preferences. This data-driven approach enables them to offer highly personalized content recommendations, leading to maximizing user engagement and retention.

3.2.2 Amazon: Dynamic Pricing and Predictive Shopping

Amazon employs AI to dynamically adjust product prices based on various factors, such as demand, competitor pricing, and customer behavior. This dynamic pricing strategy, powered by AI, contributes to increasing revenue and optimizing the online shopping experience.

This part gives a thorough investigation of the current situation with artificial intelligence in computerized promoting, exhibiting the extraordinary effect of artificial intelligence applications and giving motivation through genuine examples of overcoming adversity.

4.1 The Role of AI in Creating Personalized User Experiences

The future of AI in digital marketing is intricately linked to its role in crafting personalized user experiences. This chapter explores the pivotal role AI plays in tailoring content, products, and interactions to the unique preferences of individual users.

4.1.1 Content Personalization

AI algorithms investigation user behavior, preferences, and historical information to deliver tailored content. Whether it's personalized recommendations, individualized emails, or dynamic website content, AI-

driven personalization enhances user engagement by providing relevant and timely information.

4.1.2 Product Recommendations and E-Commerce

In the e-commerce landscape, AI-driven product recommendations are a game-changer. By understanding user preferences and purchase history, AI algorithms can suggest products that align with individual tastes, significantly influencing purchase decisions.

4.2 Importance of Data-Driven Personalization Strategies

At the heart of effective AI-driven personalization lies the utilization of data. This section delves into the significance of adopting data-driven strategies to enhance personalization in digital marketing.

4.2.1 Harnessing Customer Data

AI relies on a wealth of customer data to function effectively. Marketers must implement robust data collection and analysis mechanisms to understand user behavior, preferences, and patterns. The responsible and ethical use of this data is paramount to building trust with consumers.

4.2.2 Enhanced User Engagement and Loyalty

Personalization, powered by AI and informed by data, fosters deeper connections between brands and consumers. By delivering personalized experiences, businesses can cultivate customer loyalty, increase retention, and drive long-term value.

This chapter illuminates the future trajectory of AI in digital marketing, emphasizing the transformative impact of personalized user experiences and the central role data plays in achieving this vision. □

5.1 Exploring Predictive Analytics Powered by AI

The future landscape of digital marketing is shaped by the foresight and precision offered by predictive analytics. In this chapter, we delve into the profound impact of AI-powered predictive analytics on marketing strategies.

5.1.1 Understanding Predictive Analytics

Predictive analytics involves the use of AI algorithms to analyze historical data, identify patterns, and make informed predictions about future trends. In the context of marketing, this enables businesses to anticipate customer behaviors, market trends, and campaign outcomes.

5.1.2 Enhancing Customer Segmentation

AI-driven predictive analytics refines customer segmentation by going beyond historical data, considering current trends, and predicting future preferences. This nuanced approach ensures more accurate targeting, resulting in higher conversion rates and improved ROI.

5.2 Utilizing AI for Data-Driven Decision-Making

The integration of AI in marketing extends beyond predictive analytics, empowering data-driven decision-making processes that shape every aspect of a marketing strategy.

5.2.1 Real-Time Decision-Making

AI algorithms process vast amounts of data in real-time, enabling marketers to make decisions on the fly. This capability is particularly crucial in dynamic environments, allowing for agile responses to changing market conditions and consumer behaviors.

5.2.2 Optimization of Marketing Campaigns

From adjusting ad spending to refining content strategies, AI facilitates data-driven optimization of marketing campaigns. By continuously analyzing performance metrics and customer interactions, marketers can ensure their efforts are always aligned with evolving market dynamics.

This chapter illuminates the transformative potential of predictive analytics powered by AI and underscores the critical role of data-driven decision-making in shaping the future of digital marketing.

6.1 Understanding and Optimizing Customer Journeys Using AI

The future of digital marketing is intricately connected to the customer journey, and AI emerges as a powerful ally in comprehending and optimizing this intricate process. This chapter explores the transformative role of AI in understanding and enhancing customer journeys.

6.1.1 Comprehensive Data Analysis

AI's ability to process vast amounts of data enables a holistic understanding of the customer journey. From initial awareness to post-purchase interactions, AI algorithms analyze touchpoints and behaviors, unveiling valuable insights that guide marketers in tailoring their strategies.

6.1.2 Predictive Personalization Along the Journey

By harnessing predictive analytics, AI predicts the next steps in a customer's journey. This enables marketers to deliver personalized content, offers, and recommendations at each stage, fostering a more engaging and relevant customer experience.

6.2 Enhancing Customer Experiences Through Intelligent Mapping

AI not only aids in understanding the customer journey but also actively contributes to enhancing the overall customer experience through intelligent mapping.

6.2.1 Dynamic Content Delivery

Intelligent mapping, powered by AI, allows for dynamic content delivery based on a customer's position in their journey. This ensures that the information presented is timely, relevant, and aligned with the customer's evolving needs.

6.2.2 Proactive Engagement and Feedback

AI-driven customer journey mapping facilitates proactive engagement, enabling businesses to address customer needs before they arise. By collecting and analyzing real-time feedback, businesses can adapt their strategies in response to customer sentiments, fostering loyalty and satisfaction.

This chapter delves into the symbiotic relationship between AI and customer journey mapping, illustrating how these technologies converge to shape a future where customer experiences are not only understood but actively and intelligently optimized.

☐

7.1 Rise of AI-Powered Chabot in Customer Interactions

The future of digital marketing is witnessing a significant rise in the prominence of AI-powered Chabot. These intelligent conversational agents have transformed customer interactions, offering businesses a dynamic tool to engage with their audience.

7.1.1 Enhancing Customer Engagement

AI-powered Chabot excel in providing real-time and personalized interactions. By understanding user queries and preferences, Chabot offer immediate responses, creating a seamless and engaging customer experience.

7.1.2 Data-Driven Personalization

The integration of AI allows Chabot to analyze user data, enabling them to tailor conversations based on individual behaviors. This data-driven approach contributes to more personalized and relevant interactions, fostering stronger connections between businesses and their customers.

7.2 Implementing Conversational Marketing Strategies

As AI-powered Chabot become integral to customer interactions, businesses are leveraging conversational marketing strategies to enhance engagement and drive results.

7.2.1 Proactive Customer Outreach

Conversational marketing involves initiating real-time conversations with potential customers. AI-powered Chabot facilitate proactive outreach, enabling businesses to address customer needs, provide information, and guide them through the buyer's journey.

7.2.2 Dynamic Content Delivery

Conversational marketing is not limited to text-based interactions. AI allows Chabot to deliver dynamic content, including images, videos, and product recommendations, creating a rich and immersive conversational experience for users

This chapter explores the transformative impact of AI-powered Chabot on customer interactions and provides insights into the implementation of conversational marketing strategies, paving the way for a more engaging and personalized digital marketing landscape.

8.1 Addressing Ethical Challenges in AI-Driven Marketing

As artificial intelligence (AI) continues to shape the future of digital marketing, it brings forth a set of ethical challenges that demand careful consideration. This chapter explores the key ethical considerations associated with AI in marketing and proposes strategies to address them.

8.1.1 Bias in AI Algorithms

AI systems are susceptible to biases present in the information they are trained on, which can result in discriminatory outcomes. Addressing bias requires continuous monitoring, diverse data representation, and the development of algorithms that prioritize fairness.

8.1.2 Data Privacy and Security

The use of AI in marketing involves the collection and analysis of vast amounts of consumer data. Ensuring data privacy and security is paramount to building trust with consumers. Marketers must implement robust measures to safeguard sensitive information and adhere to data protection regulations.

8.2 Ensuring Responsible and Transparent AI Usage

To navigate the ethical landscape of AI in marketing, it is imperative to prioritize responsible and transparent usage. This section outlines principles and practices to ensure ethical AI deployment.

8.2.1 Answerable and Transparency

Marketers should strive to make AI decisions transparent and understandable. Ensuring that AI algorithms can be explained helps build trust and allows consumers to comprehend the basis for personalized recommendations and targeted advertisements.

8.2.2 Continuous Monitoring and Accountability

Implementing a system for continuous monitoring of AI algorithms is crucial. Marketers must take accountability for the impact of AI on consumer behavior and regularly assess and update algorithms to mitigate ethical risks.

This chapter serves as a guide for marketers and businesses to navigate the ethical considerations associated with AI in digital marketing, emphasizing the importance of responsible and transparent AI usage.

CHAPTER NINE

Ethical Considerations in AI Marketing - Emerging Trends and Future Innovations

9.1 Overview of Upcoming Technologies Shaping AI in Marketing

The future of artificial intelligence (AI) in digital marketing is marked by an array of emerging technologies that promise to redefine the landscape. This chapter provides an overview of these innovations and their potential impact on AI-driven marketing.

9.1.1 Augmented Reality (AR) and Virtual Reality (VR)

AR and VR technologies are poised to enhance customer experiences by creating immersive and interactive marketing campaigns. From virtual try-on experiences for products to augmented reality advertisements, these technologies hold the potential to revolutionize how brands engage with consumers.

9.1.2 Voice Search and Conversational AI

The rise of voice-activated devices and the integration of conversational AI present new opportunities and challenges. Marketers will need to adapt strategies to optimize content for voice search and leverage Chabot and virtual assistants for more natural and personalized customer interactions.

9.2 Predictions for the Future of AI-Driven Marketing

Anticipating the trajectory of AI in marketing requires insight into future trends and innovations. This section explores predictions for the evolving landscape of AI-driven marketing.

9.2.1 Hyper-Personalization

As AI algorithms become more complex, hyper-personalization will reach new heights. Marketers will leverage advanced data analytics and AI to deliver highly tailored content, products, and recommendations, enhancing customer satisfaction and engagement.

9.2.2 Ethical AI Adoption

With increasing awareness of ethical considerations, the future will witness a stronger emphasis on the ethical adoption of AI in marketing. Transparency, fairness, and accountability will be integral as businesses strive to build and maintain trust with consumers.

This chapter envisions the exciting future of AI in digital marketing, exploring emerging trends and predicting innovations that will shape the ethical landscape of AI-driven marketing.

10.1 Hands-On Guide to Implementing AI in Marketing Campaigns

This chapter serves as a practical guide for marketers looking to implement artificial intelligence (AI) in their campaigns. It provides actionable insights and step-by-step instructions to leverage AI technologies effectively.

10.1.1 Data Preparation and Integration

A crucial step in implementing AI in marketing is preparing and integrating relevant data. This section outlines best practices for collecting, cleaning, and integrating data to ensure AI algorithms receive accurate and meaningful inputs.

10.1.2 Choosing the Right AI Tools

Selecting the appropriate AI tools is essential for successful implementation. This chapter explores various AI tools and platforms available for marketing purposes, providing guidance on choosing tools that align with specific campaign objectives.

10.2 Real-World Case Studies Highlighting Successful Applications

Drawing inspiration from real-world successes, this section presents a collection of case studies showcasing how businesses have effectively implemented AI in their **marketing strategies.**

10.2.1 Personalization and Customer Engagement

Explore case studies where AI-driven personalization strategies have significantly enhanced customer engagement. Learn how businesses have used AI algorithms to deliver tailored content, product recommendations, and personalized communication.

10.2.2 Predictive Analytics in Action

Delve into examples of how predictive analytics powered by AI has transformed marketing campaigns. Understand how businesses have predicted customer behaviors, optimized targeting, and improved campaign outcomes through data-driven decision-making.

This chapter provides marketers with practical insights into implementing AI in their campaigns, offering a hands-on guide and real-world case studies that demonstrate the successful application of AI in digital marketing.